Olesia Sinkova

Freedom Fighters

story.one – Life is a story

story.one

1st edition 2023

Production, design and conception:
story.one publishing - www.story.one
A brand of Storylution GmbH

Font set from Minion Pro, Lato and Merriweather.

ISBN: 978-3-7108-4218-4

CONTENT

...

INTRO

On the 24th of February 2022 the morning for every Ukrainian began with the news that the full-scale invasion began. The peaceful reality was torn apart by bombs' explosions and the sounds of the rockets flying over our cities, this time not only in Donbass (Russian invasion there has been taking place since 2014). How does it feel to wake up in a scene of a World War II movie in the 21st century? Haven't we learned the bitter taste of destruction that war brings? The grief and pain that this machine holds for everyone involved? Haven't we as humankind realised that we have no right to take other people's lives for nothing, for the ambitious goals of some dictators? Oh, do we really need one more war, instead of working together to solve the bigger problems and build a better future for our children and grandchildren on the Earth? Or everything is so damn perfect already that there is nothing to work on in a constructive, motivating, uplifting way?

Like an electro wave the news spread among Ukrainians, abroad too. Suddenly almost the whole nation became like one family. Numb, lost, we were trying to adjust to this new reality and find our places in it. The situation Ukrainians were thrown into didn't make them victims though. Not a tiny bit of disgusting approach that Putin used, made them crawl or panic or give up. Instead of being just victims in the face of death and danger, they showed up as freedom holders, freedom fighters, as an example of humanity, compassion and courage. Back to back, hand in hand – we stand together. And it becomes dramatically vivid through the work of not only soldiers but volunteers too.

Being eager to help, I was networking a lot, and at some point, I felt like Ukraine is a country of leaders. People took personal responsibility not only for themselves, but also for those in need, who were around them. Almost everyone started "fighting on their own battlefield" – the entrepreneurs funded the humanitarian aid, or organised the humanitarian hubs, those, who had cars, were delivering food and medicine, artist and musicians were cheering people up in bomb shelters or in the underground, doctors were working, making operations in extreme conditions, without electricity sometimes, day and night without a break, café and restaurant owners were feeding those who lost their homes, and thousands and thousands of ordinary people started to volunteer.

Volunteers are superheroes who can find ANYTHING ANYWHERE and deliver within hours or days, breaking all logical rules of this material world. Would soldiers need a car or some facility, it seems like volunteers can get it all with the help of hundreds of ordinary people. I hope I am not romanticising this. The lesson the war is teaching us is a very expensive one. It cost us as a humanity millions of broken lives and millions of lives taken away. We are one, and we won't manage to build a safe, prosperous environment globally until we learn this lesson and start to behave accordingly, on a very personal level. My single story is a drop in a huge ocean of strength, devotion, faith and courage. But we are all just drops in a huge ocean of humanity. Yet together we can create a meaningful wave of change by keeping up, showing up for each other, investigating and doing our best to remain a conscious leader even in our small area of responsibility.

"When an unexpected change happens to us, it can also inspire a lasting change within us."
– Dr. Maya Shankar

ESCAPE

"We are living in 15 minutes, pack the most important things", – my husband rushed into the room. It was a firm decision, with no space for hesitation, but my mind ran a mile with anxious thoughts before I could accept this fact. We are leaving. Right now. It was the 12th day of a full-scale Russian invasion of Ukraine, the 12th day since someone decided to start it all over again – the rivers of blood and tears, spreading death and fear, putting another dreadful and stupid mark on humankind, still playing those power games by means of other people's lives, leaving another unbearable scar onto humanity's heart. Didn't they learn History at school? It's basic!

With three small kids – 3, 5 and 7 – we couldn't take much, the evacuation trains were not taking suitcases or anything big, just backpacks and handbags. And people's lives, which were way more important. Where are we heading to? I have a cousin in Germany, so I called her while my mind was caught up in a turmoil of thoughts: "Can we come?" I don't even know where we would be if not for her words: "Come, you will get help here".

It was hard to leave your whole life behind, but we sensed – it wouldn't be over very soon. Being born in Lugansk, and knowing the whole story of the Russian invasion of Donbass since 2014 gave me a quick blink into what to expect. In therapy, you let go of your old life slowly, bringing emotions to the surface. But we didn't have time – life was asking to let go right here, right now, accepting the fact, that it would never be the same again.

Our train was at night. There was no fixed schedule, everything depended on the situation, some rails were destroyed by bombs or rockets and then the trains were changing the route to keep the passengers safe. It was cold. March, but still winter outside. Evacuation trains were free but full. Full like no place to stand even. And you had to travel the whole country across to reach the other side (and it is 1,316 km). Sometimes the conductors would not even open the doors, then people would need to wait for the next evacuation train to try their luck. We were lucky at the first try. We got on board and the kids even had some place to sleep. When an air-raid siren was crying loud into the dark sky, the blood was running cold in my veins. I think 2022 was the year everyone learned to pray, even atheists.

When we got to our destination – it was crowded. We had to wait in a very long queue to get on a local train to cross the border with Poland. Hours and hours of *waiting* underground, and at the same time some people were *living* in the underground in Kharkiv and Kyiv, and even giving birth to their children there, in such conditions that no one has ever thought we as a civilization, would have to go through again.

Poland welcomed us with normal life, and it was healing for our nervous systems. A wave of gratitude covered us from head to toe, and soaking up the peaceful environment we fell asleep in a cosy room of a hotel, to leave for Berlin the next day. Germany would be our final stop, where trust in kindness and beauty of people's hearts would not only be restored, but also engraved forever in our souls.

*"Trauma creates change you don't choose.
Healing is about creating change you do choose."*
– Michelle Rosenthal

"Wear your vulnerability with pride. That's what makes us human."
– Misan Harriman

YOGA AND WAR

We arrived at daytime, not believing the long way was over. We are safe. There is nothing to worry about right at this moment – just enjoy the warm hugs from the people you love, feel at home again, in a no-war reality. Enjoy the shower, the blue sky and home-made food. When we got to a safe place, reunited with my relatives – my psyche felt safe … for a breakdown. A long month of psychological pain began for me – I was crying at nights, couldn't sleep, was very sensitive and didn't know why on earth I was doing all this right at the moment when everything seemed to be so nice and so nourishing. It took me weeks of my personal practice (breath work, yoga and meditation), with the help of my friend, to feel like I can handle my life again, and that my emotions were no longer an ocean ready to swallow me. I realised how vital emotional balance was. Even when you might have everything to be happy and satisfied, your tired psyche can play an awful joke on you, leaving you unable to enjoy all the abundance you have at your disposal.

There is no practical way to be productive when you are overwhelmed with hard feelings and e-motions, and I knew the tools how to balance all that.

So I applied for a scholarship at Kundalini Research Institute and took a course to become a real yoga teacher, to be able to help other people to free themselves from the emotional baggage that can make their life unbearable. My desire to show up for other people was also fuelled by all the kindness and care that we received here, in Germany, from my cousin and her family to absolute strangers, who were gifting us clothes, furniture and other stuff necessary for living. Yes, we came almost empty-handed, and we would really not manage without the other people's help. As in that film, "Pay It Forward", 2000, my only wish was to spread this flow of kindness forward. So straight after the course I offered a free online circle of support for Ukrainian refugees all over the world. We were meeting twice a week, were practicing yoga and meditation together, talking, helping each other and creating this sense of a heartfelt community, where everyone could arrive as he or she is, with all the feelings and emotions, challenges and problems in order to feel – I am not alone and I can manage. It was my priority to do all I could to help people find peace at least within their own minds and bodies, finding a way to deal with pressure and stress and building up courage and trust to their own selves, to their capabilities and inner resources.

Sudden shocking events can influence people in two ways – whether shut them down and lead to depressive states or ignite a spark of spirit awakening and bring people to a whole new level of their own capabilities and perception of life. Writing this book I didn't want to share just my own story, I wanted to be a voice for those volunteers, who are helping others even under shelling, who don't have time to write, because of constant stress, who are not safe, who are risking, who are helping in extreme conditions and those who find an opportunity to help even being thousands kilometres away. Some stories were not told because of volunteers' burnout, and many will already never be told. So I collected the stories within my reach, edited and somehow compressed them to share with you, so that they could be seen and heard. Because they truly matter. Here they are.

"When you reach the end of what you should know, you will be at the beginning of what you should sense."

– Kahlil Gibran

ANGELS ON EARTH

Iren Brynza, 34, a photographer, educator, artist, Chernihiv, Ukraine, @iren.brynza:

On February 24th, 2022, my husband and I woke up to a call from a relative, who was in the military, and he said we should evacuate to Western Ukraine. We did so but after a while we still returned to Chernihiv because we wanted to be of help. I started volunteering in the kitchen of a volunteer centre, cooking for soldiers, sorting and packing humanitarian aid, fundraising etc. I was also active in the local chats where requests for help were posted daily. I remember one request from a mom and her child who needed evacuation – they asked if anyone could drive them to a bomb shelter, and I remember this impulse I felt that I had to do it straight away. So I drove them, and the next day there was an explosion right near their house, which didn't have any kind of bomb shelter or any secure place to hide. I realised that that powerful urge to help them right away was something guiding me, a higher power, which I thought to be the guardian angel of this child. After all, those were just the people from my city, I had never met them before.

There are many stories like this to tell, these are just some of them. I remember how we went to Chernivtsy to buy some ammunition. I was somewhere in the city and there was a girl who came up to me and hugged me with tears in her eyes and said, "Thank you so much, you saved my mom's life!" And this was a really emotional moment for me; I'd already felt like giving up volunteering, but this encounter showed me that I had to keep on doing what I was doing.

One day I was delivering some medications across the city of Chernihiv. I was on my way to an old woman with some heart disease medication she needed when they stopped me at a checkpoint, just a mere moment before the air-raid siren set off and the shells started to burst. A military man shouted something at me, I couldn't understand him, got nervous and, to make matters worse, my seat belt got jammed and wouldn't unlock. This all lasted for about 5 minutes or so, but in the end I just decided to drive on. I came to the house where I was supposed to be 5 minutes before, and what I saw was that it had been massively shelled and if it wasn't for that 5-minute mess at the checkpoint, I would have been there, in that place. I realised that I could have been killed right then and there. It was a very intense moment for me and I felt like I'd died and come back to life again.

Or another time we were in a volunteer centre, sorting the medications and then suddenly we heard the shell bursting and the window blowing out. I saw that the cupboard with medications was falling down right on me and the first thought that came to my mind was, "Oh no, I have to keep it in one place", because the medications had already been sorted and we'd got many urgent requests for them, so I didn't worry that we would be blown up with this house right that moment, I worried about medications.

All these stories, both funny and horrifying, didn't make me feel like my life was on the edge. It was more like a quest, when you don't realise the danger you are in, and instead you just have new tasks and you keep searching for clues and guidance, and move forward fearlessly.

"In the midst of the darkness,
grab a flashlight."
– Gabrielle Bernstein

THE UNIVERSE GOT OUR BACKS

Ilona Strona, 38, an entrepreneur, investor, Kyiv, Ukraine, @ilonastrona:

I got into volunteering because I felt I could organise people and be useful to them. And, frankly, it was also a way to distract myself from the terrible news. All my energy was directed towards coordinating, organising the logistics of getting people out of Kyiv, Kharkiv, and other cities that were under massive shelling. Together with other volunteers, we were finding cars and helping people who needed evacuation, we were searching for accommodations too. By teaming up, we were able to be more productive in helping people to get out of dangerous places and find some accommodation as well. We created a chat where we could connect those who were looking for help with those who could provide it.

Among all the different stories, I especially remember this one. We were expecting some vital medications from another city to arrive, but because of the curfew, we just couldn't go and pick them up. There was a girl whose life depended on those medications, so we couldn't just give up and with the help of a group of volunteers, through thorough coordination and synchronising our efforts, we managed to pick up the pills in Gaisin and finally gave them to the girl. There were tears of joy as everything worked out in the end, we managed to save a life.

Another story worth remembering is this one, where every life mattered. When the news broke out that the tanks were already close, my friend's mother was on the left bank of Kyiv. There were 17 of us and 2 cars ready to go, but my friend didn't want to leave without her mother and brother. Somehow, we managed to find one more car, right on the left bank, to pick our people up and everything worked out in a miraculous way, so we all were able to leave. I admit, it was hard, travelling with so little space in a car, but that just showed humanity as we didn't leave anyone behind. And it didn't matter that among all those people there were some I met the first time then.

I have friends who set up a charity fund "Oseredok" and we used to go to Poland and bring cars for our armed forces. The guys are amazing and often go to the places where help is extremely needed. Not only that, the house I live in has so many caring people. After the Kakhovska hydroelectric power station had been bombed, we collected clothes with my neighbours and sent them over to Kherson through the charity fund.

“Do what you can with what you have wherever you are.”
– Theodore Roosevelt

FIGHTING WITH ANY WEAPONS WE HAVE

Elina Ellis, 42, an illustrator, author, educator, Cambridge, UK / Zaporizhzhia, Ukraine, @elinaellis:

I've been living in England for 22 years or so, but I am Ukrainian and my connections to Ukraine are very strong. When the war started my heart got broken into a thousand pieces. I could scream from horror and helplessness. I was ready to give everything I could to help, if only it could help. But that was just the initial shock. Then I started to think – what I can ACTUALLY do, no matter how small.

First, I donated all the money I had in my Ukrainian bank account to the army. That was easy to do with just one click. Then I searched for any volunteer organisations in Cambridge, where I live, and found one that was connecting British sponsors to Ukrainian refugees and organising their safe arrival and settlement in England. I signed up straight away and was involved in relocating people for the first several months of the war, the time when no one really knew what to do and where to go. It was a very rewarding job. I felt like I was making a difference, at least to the people I was working with. This job kept reassuring me that love, care, kindness still exist in the world.

I also have a small educational business, selling lectures and masterclasses about children's illustration. Ever since the first days of the war, we decided to donate half of our earnings to the charity in Zaporizhzhya, organised by my friend. She is buying medicine needed to save the lives of Ukrainian children who were injured by Russian soldiers.

My other friend is helping homeless cats in Berdiansk, which is now an occupied territory. At the moment she has 200 cats living with her in a three bedroom apartment. They all need feeding and looking after. Me and another artist from Cambridge are making sure the cats have what they need with regular donations.

I also draw illustrations for free for any charity trying to help Ukraine in any possible way. I support any businesses or producers that allocate a portion of their earnings to Ukrainian charities.

I don't think that I am doing much. I know plenty of people who are giving much more and doing much more. But I believe that if all of us do what we can to help Ukraine, she will stand and she will win this wretched war.

Because each of us, Ukrainians, whether at home or abroad, are now fighting our own war. The war with ignorance, cruelty, absurdity and darkness. We are fighting this war with any weapons we have. With donations, with volunteer's work, with kindness and support to those in need, with demonstrations and public appeals, with words, songs, art, or just with HOPE that keeps living in our hearts. We are fighting with belief in our country, in our people, in our army, in freedom and democratic values.

"I thank whatever gods may be
For my unconquerable soul."
– William Ernest Henley

MIRACLES

Alla Titova, 40, a primary school teacher, founder and director of a children's camp, Zaporizhzhia / Kyiv, Ukraine, @alampika777:

Kyiv was under heavy shelling and was slowly turning into a ghost town. There were no cars or people on the streets. The terrible silence of a big empty city... I couldn't help but think if there was anything I could do to help. One evening I heard the terrible news that a convoy of civilians travelling from Mariupol to Zaporizhzhia had been ruthlessly shot, that there were many victims, including children. Later on I saw a horrifying video from the children's regional intensive care unit showing children from Mariupol and Zaporizhzhia region being severely injured. I had very good friends in that department, so the same day I contacted them and learned about the needs of the department and how we could support the families of these children. I received a list of necessary things and I just wrote a post about it. And so many people responded! I was amazed at how many people were ready to help, feeling united. I did not expect it at all. Friends and strangers from Zaporizhzhia and other cities called me, offered their help, and friends and strangers transferred money. Our donations covered the needs of the hospital in just one day! This made me realise that together we can do much more!

The first kids we were taking care of were Milena, a 10-year-old girl, who was shot in the cheek after passing the checkpoint, 5-year-old Vladik, who was wounded by a bullet in the stomach while evacuating from the war zone in Zaporizhzhia region by car. There was also Artemka, who received bullet wounds during the evacuation from Mariupol, and Dima, whose family was in a shelter in Mariupol, but after a massive explosion he and his father received shrapnel wounds. They were all in critical condition. Although I wasn't there, I knew for sure that together with my friends and family who stayed in Zaporizhzhia, we would be able to purchase and deliver everything they needed. The most difficult thing for me was to find courage to call the parents of these children and offer help gently, finding the right words of support. I had no idea what people who had gone through this horror could feel. But somehow I found the right words, they opened their hearts, accepted help, however hard it was for some to even realise that they needed it. In a moment, these people lost everything. Not only that, they almost lost the most valuable people in their lives – their children. But they managed through! The children put up a great struggle for life. They inspired us to never stop and to do even more. I cried every day seeing that we were able to help and make a change together! We started as strangers, but we became a strong team.

Thank you, Dmytro Tkalych, Iryna Dyachenko, Tatiana Leleka, Elina Ellis, Victoria Velichko and everyone who participated in our work. During this year we've collected more than hundreds of thousands hryvnias for medications, we've helped displaced people with housing, work, clothes, food and, most importantly, made all these people feel they were not alone in this plight! I could not even imagine that we were so united, that we could count on such powerful support. For me, all this is a real MIRACLE. We will overcome it together! Strong, sincere, unbreakable! Glory to Ukraine!

"For what you do to others, you do to yourself."
– Eckhart Tolle

FOR FAMILY

Ekateryna Pereverzeva, 37, a personal stylist, Kyiv / Mariupol, Ukraine, @katya.style:

When the war began, I was filled with anxiety, but yet I hoped it would finish soon. I wanted to help other people, but didn't know exactly how. That's why I began re-posting endless Instagram stories about those, who were asking for help and from those, who could provide help. We were still in Kyiv at that time. I still was able to call and talk to my parents, who live in Mariupol (later this city was massively attacked, occupied by Russian army and citizens were kept in unbearable conditions). Then, one day a rocket flew very close to our house, the plaster fell off a wall in some places, and we realised it was time to go to Western Ukraine for safety reasons. It took us 4 days to get to Lviv, we were staying for a night in churches or wherever it was possible to spend a night in. There were huge queues on the roads. It was the first time mobile connection with my parents started to disappear. And when we got to our final destination, it was blocked and the worst weeks of my life began. My personal hell. I didn't know if they were alive, what happened to them. All of my relatives were in Mariupol at that time. All of them. So, when we were finally in Lviv, I decided to give my full attention, my heart to volunteering, to serving people, full-heartedly. When you have such kind of intention, the Universe starts to support you. The moment I went out from our car as we arrived in Lviv, I met my old acquaintance who had come here earlier from Kyiv too and had been already volunteering – in a volunteer centre "Asgard". They were just starting off, so they needed new people badly. One problem was solved. This woman also helped us with accommodation, which was a real problem there, as there were either no flats available, or the rent was just as high as for a mention in Las Vegas.

Volunteering was saving me from constant painful thoughts about what was going on in Mariupol. We had so much to do, I didn't have a spare minute, but it was only during the day-time. At night, when I was coming home from the volunteer center, the horror of reality was hitting me back again, as I was trying to reach my family, but their numbers were no longer working, because the Russian army occupied our city. I spent three weeks like that. I kept sane only because of volunteering. I was escaping from my own anxiety by doing something meaningful. The people, who were around me, the help we managed to provide together, real deeds, real actions – all this was keeping me alive. We created “Pryhystok” – a safe place for refugees to stay. I was also responsible for sending humanitarian aid from Lviv to Kharkiv and one of my tasks was to find drivers who would deliver 10-20 tonnes of humanitarian aid to Kharkiv for free. Eventually we sent almost 10 or more 20-tonne lorries to Kharkiv to support people there.

My service to people was a way to ask God to protect my family and help them stay alive. My volunteering was devoted to their lives. Later, I started to receive some messages about my family   they were alive, in unbearable conditions but alive. And I gradually started to calm down. At the same time the amount of humanitarian aid we were receiving and working with started to reduce. So eventually we returned to Kyiv, but I still help volunteer centres by donating 10% from any income I get.

"Only when it is dark enough,
can you see the stars."
– Martin Luther King, Jr.

SHINE YOUR LIGHT

Victoria Moskovchenko, 26, an English teacher, Chernihiv, Ukraine, @victoriia_mos:

I was born and raised in the glorious city of Chernihiv, a heroic city. This city, though small, showed its love for Ukraine, the power of our people and its tremendous resistance to the Russian army on February 24th (the day of the full-scale invasion).

I started volunteering right away. At first, my sister and I were Ministry of Health hotline assistants, where we were processing requests from our people who needed medications because not all pharmacies were open. In three days it went from all the drug stores operating normally, to only some of them, and then, to none of them being open. Unfortunately, not all people were provided with enough medications and not everyone managed to receive them. This is a cruel war against civilians.

And then the people, who I have been friends with for more than 5 years, initiated a support project - British Camp Supports @britishcamp.supports. Unfortunately, their camp and school were destroyed by Russian troops in the city of Irpin.

At first, we helped and covered the most basic needs – food, medicine, hygiene products. Every day we were receiving 50 or 100 requests. It was hard, but we helped everyone. We listened to their stories, cried but kept on working because we knew that all this was not in vain. Before the school year, we helped the children with school supplies. And in winter, we ran a New Year Present Appeal where people could buy New Year presents for children. With the help of other volunteers, we also sent blankets to some families living in modular housing units. Other families needed help with reinstalling their windows. It was cold. And it was dark. Yet it was bright because we have people with pure light inside their hearts.

Now we have changed our forms of assistance: we provide emotional support, and we help to rebuild and furnish the houses that were damaged. We have already helped some families and now we have launched a fundraiser to rebuild the house of another family, who has gone through too much suffering over these dark days. As of now, we have processed more than 900 requests. And we have seen tears in the eyes of those we helped…

I am proud that we have so many people who are courageous, sincere, always ready to help, restore and rebuild. It is often said that in dark times, you can see bright people. And I have seen them. And I am proud to have grown up and live here.

*"Start by doing what's necessary;
then do what's possible; and
suddenly you are doing the
impossible."*
– Francis of Assisi

UA-FEST

Oleksandra Burtseva, 42, a lawyer, owner of a children's centre, Dnipro, Ukraine, @shooshe4ka

I am a Russian-speaking Ukrainian with Jewish roots and there is an interesting fact weaved into the history of our family. In 1943, my great-grandmother Esther, took her sons and fled from her native Dnipro to Kokand, Uzbekistan, because of Nazis. And in 2022, my mother Esther, took my sister and me, and we took our children and we were forced to flee from our native Dnipro to Germany, because of Russian nazis. Such a twist of fate.

I don't consider myself as a volunteer, but since the Russian invasion in 2014, I have been helping as much as I could, mostly doctors.

At the beginning of the war, before our forced emigration, having acquaintances in many spheres, my friends and I organised fleece, cutting, sewing, delivery of balaclavas and thermal underwear to the military, and at the same time we organised sewing of underwear for the wounded in hospitals.

When my sons and I were evacuated to Germany, I organised and conducted creative classes with refugee children here on the platform of the "Ukraine" project from the Deutsches Fußballmuseum, while collecting aid for the military and sending it to the volunteers in D-nipro.

My biggest volunteer project here is UA-FEST or #friedensfest, organised together with the same museum on 27.08.2022 in honour of the Independence Day of Ukraine. 9 hours of work of the museum, food courts and a fair with Ukrainian dishes, souvenirs, clothes, a fashion show and sale of collections of Ukrainian designers, a concert with the participation of Ukrainian bands and a Kharkiv rock orchestra, together gathered a record number of visitors for a Ukrainian event. The locations organised by the refugees collected 8900 euros of aid, which was transferred to the account of the Ukrainian Charitable Foundation and used to support Ukrainians. Also, the entire profit of the museum on that day (15000 euros) was donated to the Klitschko brothers' initiative to support and develop sports talent in Ukraine.

Now I continue my volunteer work in Germany, because I believe that this is my contribution to bringing our Victory closer and making my coming back home possible.

“Leadership is a choice, not a rank. It’s choosing to look out for the person on your left and to look out for the person on your right.”

– Simon Sinek

PREVENTING BURNOUTS

Olena Ostapchuk, 41, a civil society activist, PhD, Zhytomyr, Ukraine:

In 2014, when Russia started the war against Ukraine, I was pregnant, and in March of the same year I gave birth to my son. Now Artem is 9 years old, and all these years our country has been fighting against Russian tyranny. When you give birth to a child, you especially want security, peace, home comfort, and a calm course of life, but these attributes of a happy life were all taken away. On 4 March 2022, the lyceum where my son studied was destroyed by a Russian missile. At first, in a state of shock, you cannot believe your own eyes, your brain refuses to accept reality... On the same day, it became obvious that I had to evacuate my child abroad, because there was no safe place in Ukraine. I left my job at the university, projects at an NGO, we left the house we had built, we left our family, our son separated from his father for the first time. We drove through settlements that no longer had signs with their names to disorient the enemy. My son and I were crossing the Polish border on foot with two suitcases, standing in a long queue. It was cold outside, we met children and women who were lightly dressed, they had no time to pack because they were leaving their homes in a hurry. Frightened and cold, the war forced us abroad.

Once I was in Germany and realised that my child was in a safe environment despite the enormous stress, I decided to take care of those who care about others. My focus was on my colleagues from the NGO "Parytet". In Zhytomyr, women from our organisation were volunteering, trying to help, exhausted, with pain in their backs after unloading humanitarian supplies. From our short conversations, it became clear to me that they would burn out very quickly. Helping others, they had a lot of unmet needs of their own, which they were very careful to mention. They were worried about food security, health issues, three of our activists were pregnant, total uncertainty and danger took away the rest of their strength. So I decided to write an application for a project to cover the basic needs and support our activists. I wasn't doing anything extraordinary, I was doing what I knew how to do. I know how to write grant applications and implement projects because I've been doing it for the last 15 years as a civil society activist. However, this initiative was unique in that the target audience was female civil society activists and volunteers of our organisation, i.e. the people who were usually the project implementers. The project was funded by the Urgent Action Fund for Women's Human Rights (UAF). The grant met the practical needs of the activists of the NGO "Parytet". These include medical examinations and the purchase of medicines; food security (purchase of the necessary equipment for food preparation and storage (heating dehumidifier, vacuum sealer, high-pressure electric autoclave, kitchen machine); purchase of essential goods for the newborn children of our activists; hygiene needs (hygiene products, household chemicals). Thanks to the timely support and prevention of professional burnout, the activists of our NGO were able to continue their work to promote and protect women's rights in wartime. And my main message is that it is important to support those who support others.

"Thinking will not overcome fear
but action will."
– W. Clement Stone

TRANSFORMATION

Dmytro Tyzhnenko, 39, a software developer, Kharkiv, Ukraine, @tyzhnenko.dmytro:

My story of "transformation" from whoever I was before into a volunteer begins on the morning of February 24th, 2022. For many in Ukraine, that morning divided their lives into before and after. We woke up to the building shaking and saw a red glow on the horizon from the rocket launches. We learned what was happening from the news. It took me a while to comprehend what was going on in the country. We packed quickly to the sound of gunshots and explosions and fled to our friends, to be in a safer place after two days of driving. We made our first donations to the military straight away, all while being on our way there; as soon as we arrived, we started to help the local foundations and volunteers who were collecting food and things for the displaced people or sending humanitarian aid to the cities near the front. My personal savings started to run out, so I was searching for other ways to help too. I joined some volunteer groups and started exploring my options and learning a whole new process. I defined that my way to make a contribution was to do fundraising and buy technical devices needed for our soldiers. In fact, this is what I still do in between my work and family. That said, I still had many questions and fears inside, like 'How is it done?' or 'Who will trust me with their money and why should they?'

My first fundraising still remains dear to me not only because I was doing it for the first time, but also because it saved lives. It was in March, the Ukrainian warehouses were empty, we organised a fundraiser for some Chinese walkie-talkies for our soldiers, which they'd planned to have as a backup. The ones they were using were unsecured and anyone could listen in on the transmissions, including the enemy. Fundraising went slower than expected, so I had to invest my own savings, but I never regretted that. And here's why. Once, this military unit came under fire while performing a task and there were many wounded. A soldier who was conscious tried to call for reinforcements and medical assistance, but found his main walkie-talkie damaged by the debris, so it was not working. And that was the moment when one of our walkie-talkies came in very handy, because the soldier was able to ask for medical help and, as a result, save the wounded. For me personally, this was worth all my efforts and money for this fundraising.

There was another story, a sad one unfortunately, that has really left the mark on me. The team that I joined in the first weeks of the war had a girl, Yana "Yara" Rykhlitskaya. Despite the danger, she was delivering aid to the military who were at the front in hot spots. We didn't know each other personally, and only exchanged chat messages. Despite this, she was part of the team for me, part of us. Then she quit volunteering to serve in the Armed Forces of Ukraine. She was engaged in saving lives as a combat medic. Unfortunately, she died during the evacuation of the wounded. This left a heavy imprint on all of us, but the enemy still exists, and we need to keep on working. She still inspires and motivates us all to continue our resistance and hasten victory!

I would like to thank everyone who pursues this aim, especially to all the women and men in the Armed Forces of Ukraine. Thank you for your service!

"There's nothing stronger than
the heart of a volunteer!"
– Lt. Col. Jimmy Doolittle,
"Pearl Harbor"

GIRLS ARE ALSO INVOLVED...

Marianna Kolesnikova, 38, an entrepreneur, Kyiv, Ukraine:

Before this war I used to do my favourite thing in life. I had my own business. I used to take groups of people to various exotic countries: Africa, Latin America, Japan, Korea, etc. But since 24th of February 2022, it has changed and the trips I made were not that positive and exciting, but very meaningful. At first, we fled to Irpin with friends, all we could do was just monitor the news. It was actually not my thing, just sitting and watching, so I started volunteering almost straight away. Soon, I was managing one of the volunteer hubs on the left bank of the Dnieper. Then it became more like a commercial organisation, so I left. The connections I had made in three months gave me the opportunity to meet a wonderful Ukrainian man who came from Germany (he has been living there for more than 20 years). He needed someone to organise the process. First, we went to Bucha. From May 2022 to February 2023, we volunteered together. For the most part, we wanted to help the military. Because we both understood what was the price Ukrainians were paying for justice to be done. The last trip was planned to Lyman, where we managed to congratulate almost 1700 children from the Lyman district (Chasiv Yar and Bakhmut) on St. Nicola's Day. At the same time, we opened two resilience centres and provided the women in the military with new warm jackets, because there were places with no electricity, and it was -25 C. It was a very exhausting and very interesting trip. I was already involved in serving in the military, too.

What I saw in war zones always made me think (and still does): "What else should be done to stop this?" I was selected for three different units, and there were only two important things to me – the commander's motivation should resonate with mine and his or her humanity mattered. That's how I joined the unit where I am now. There are 8 girls in it. Almost all of them are pilots. My task is to be the "eyes" of the operation. And for the first three weeks I was sleeping 1.5 hours a day. It's hard to be here, on the battlefield. Sometimes it is very hard for me and I feel ashamed of it, because there are those who are in a more difficult situation.

It's hard to see the whole picture. And sometimes it's even harder to see the details. The whole picture is this: terrible fighting, with a lot of wounded and dead, when there are not enough shells at a certain moment, when you are hit by bombs 10 times a day, and you don't drink much so you don't have to go to the toilet which is outside. It's hard to see the ruined cities where people used to live. There is nothing left in them. Nothing at all. You also see the deaths of your comrades online. It's painful.

But here I am among my people. I have met a lot of good people since the beginning of my service. Sometimes we laugh, sometimes we cry together, united by the same goal. Sometimes we are scared together. And everyone is just the way they are. I do not regret joining the military, because I understand that I could not have done it otherwise. My volunteer friend, by the way, joined the military right after me. And I am very proud of him, although I am very worried. I have a very interesting life, I think. Not boring for sure!

"Alone we can do so little;
together we can do so much."
– Helen Keller

NETWORK OF CONNEC-TIONS

Oleksiy Guzenko, 31, a back developer, Kyiv, Ukraine, @lehag92:

We were in Kyiv, when the war began, the same day we were already on a 12-hour trip in one long traffic jam to Zhytomyr. The first month we were just adjusting to the shock and were doing our best to keep on working in a 2-bedroom apartment with 7 people in. I started volunteering myself on April 11th, 2022 for my uncle, fundraising for a 4x4 pickup truck for his military unit. It was successful, though I had no previous experience in volunteering and had never thought of it. This time I didn't have a choice, so I started with what I had – my money, my network of friends and professional contacts and some Telegram chats. My knowledge about cars was limited to understanding that there were pickups and ordinary cars. Looking through the prices for such cars I accepted the fact that I would pay either the whole sum or the biggest part of it myself. I was ashamed to ask people around, even the closest ones. Quite quickly, we found a pickup in Romania and the price was great, the owner even helped to deliver it to the border. And then a beautiful choreography of networking, connecting people, reaching out, finding right places to have services done began. So the car was driven to Zhytomyr, painted, checked, repaired without me even seeing it or touching it. I was doing what I was good at – communicating and making connections. Later there were three more cars bought and delivered to our soldiers.

I also saw that a former colleague was actively participating in a newly created charity foundation "Volyn in action". I helped them a little financially, and after a while they helped me with shoes for my uncle's unit. Around the same time, a classmate of my wife returned from a battlefield with a concussion, he told us what his division needed. So, we managed to help them with not expansive requests (uniforms, thermal underwear, tactical gloves etc.) During the first months, it was difficult to get special devices in Ukraine, I was able to find some really useful mini computers though. Similarly, using my network of connection, I was able to get 10 pieces of uniforms for my uncle's division for free from colleagues abroad. In general through my connections we managed to buy cars, drones, thermal scopes. Some things were sponsored by funds, like shoes, soft water canisters, tactical first aid kits, 30 kg of medicine, tile carrier, 3 boxes of socks, 20 more boxes of medicine, power banks, blocks, cables, and much much more. But it just highlights, who we all can help using our strengths and our network of connections.

During my volunteering work I realised that my strongest skills were leading negotiations and, probably, taking risks (not always, though). My persistence and desire to make best deals not only saved money in some situations, buying expensive drones, for example, but also proved how much we could do together, just using our network of friends and existing connections. ~2 million UAH was collected and spent in name of our Victory in such a way.

"We don't even know how strong we are until we are forced to bring that hidden strength forward."

– Isabel Allende

RESCUE NOW

Vlad Glavacheck, 33, a salesperson, Kharkiv, Ukraine, @glavacheck:

As the Russian full-scale invasion of Ukraine began, many people started volunteering, and I was no exception. At first, I was sitting in the basement of my club and didn't know what to do. The only option then was monitoring social media, where I saw many requests for help. I was inspired by my friends and other people, who were already helping around, and I was really afraid to die in a meaningless way, scared just to be pinned down by the building's tiles or stitched by shell fragments, without having done anything useful. So I thought it was a great time to set an example of decent behaviour and to create stories to remember. I made my first step, posting, that I would help buy needed things and feed people. I started searching for contacts and making phone calls. It helped me to stay sane in the basement. Plus, when you start diving into the process, you have more control over the situation. And with the first successes, more energy and strength arrived.

Later, when my parents and I left Kharkiv (it was early March), I was tormented by the fact that I was leaving but so many people stayed and needed help. When we were in Lviv, I just got out of the car with my backpack, truly stepping into the unknown. This was the beginning of an adventure. After giving myself some time to think, I decided to get back to Kharkiv. With the help of Igor Klyuchnik, I reached Misha Chernomorets, the head of the "Molodost" restaurant. They were constantly evacuating people from Kharkiv to Dnipro and coming back with food and fuel. So I joined them. It was a bit shocking when you could enter a supermarket in Dnipro and buy food, while only 200 km away there were queues of 200-300 people near supermarkets waiting to buy products, but there were only cognac and cigarettes on the shelves.

We filled the car with food and drove to Kharkiv. The road was empty. When we drove into Kharkiv, there was a battle in the air over the city, and one of the planes was shot down. We already arrived almost under curfew and were stopped at a checkpoint. We stayed for about an hour and a convoy came to pick us up. With no lights on, we were driving through darkness. Something was burning, something was crashed, something was periodically exploding in different parts of the city, there were trolleybus wires hanging down, flashing city lights, scattered stones, ground everywhere, battered facades...

...Everything was exploding around us, and we were standing against the wall of the transformer. Someone was smoking and watching, listening to the enemy plane flying over the city. Soon we were escorted to the Central Department Store building. It was "Molodist" restaurant – our hub in the basement. Misha is entrepreneur, so he thought like an entrepreneur. We needed to set up a warehouse, supply chain, system, and so on. That's what I did. There were 80 people, tonnes of humanitarian aid, a kitchen and an enormous amount of requests for help. So I stayed there, on the tiles of one of the cold premises for the next 6 months. Now it is a large fund "Rescue Now".

"The difference between what we do and what we are capable of doing would suffice to solve most of the world's problems."
– Mahatma Gandhi

STRONGER THAN CIRCUM-STANCES

Vlad Glovacheck (continuation):

I became the head of the hub "Rescue Now". At first, I was just laying everything down, and then I started to organise it. When I arrived, the basement was packed to the top with food from Europe. During the day there were tens of cars coming, delivering products. There were mountains of humanitarian aid. We barely had time to unload. So, I started building a system. Started to sort everything. We developed technological maps, set up logistics routes and integrated a program for building them. We hired pharmacists. Assigned roles. It was difficult to build a system because every day something was changing. The people you relied on were leaving. And all this under constant pressure, lack of sleep, calls for help, stress. There were a lot of problems, but I liked it. Thanks to the system, the new people I was hiring, were able to understand what to do in 10 minutes. We also sorted everything by composition. I like to make the most of my limited resources. We delivered about 100,000 packages in almost six months of the active phase of combat operations in the city, it's about 16,000 packages per month and almost 500 packages per day.

When things got better and food was no longer the major problem, I left in search of some more urgent tasks. At that time, a doctor friend of mine suggested that I take up military and civilian rehabilitation. I didn't know a thing about it, but sure I was in. I think I'm an adventurer by nature. I like to dive into chaos and the unknown. So I contacted a number of funds, but I got only one response – it was the charity foundation "Citizen". They had been helping for a long time already. They did prosthetics and operations. I contacted the medical director and the first task I got was a challenging one. I had to find an ophthalmologist abroad for a military man whose chance to save the eye was little. But the mission was accomplished. I started building momentum. I was helping the wounded with appointments and consultations; the doctors with resources. I applied all the negotiation skills I had and they worked well. I also joined a medical mission stillstrongua.com and helped them with the site, presentation, organised their work. This is a Ukrainian-American facial reconstruction mission. There were times they were doing about 35 facial surgeries a week. They were starting at 7 a.m. and finishing at 11 p.m.

I have many conclusions about this experience. I appreciate it. How I was avidly melting the ore of challenges. I like it when it requires your wit, and you have to find the solutions. It made me a better person. It gave me experience, energy and confidence. Volunteering is an opportunity to explore yourself and learn a lot. I now understand why this experience is very much appreciated abroad where there is more of this culture. It's a culture of getting up and doing something. Doing something just because you can. There is a great potential hidden in a person and everyone can do much more than they expect from themselves. So you just need to dive into these circumstances and test your God. If your intentions are pure, then everything will work out. A person is stronger than the circumstances.

CONCLUSION

True leadership is simple. You just take responsibility and choose to care for someone to the right of you, someone to the left of you and just anyone within your reach. By doing something for the benefit of all, at least in our own circle of responsibilities, for people within our reach, we create a better world for ourselves and for those who are around. But what life would be if this became a way of living for everyone? Would wars still exist? I honestly believe big changes in our global community will never be made alone. Only together we can really make a difference.

That's why I think that Ukraine is a country of leaders. I shared only some stories of volunteers I knew or worked with (let the rest of the stories make a new book!) just because I had this chance and I wanted to create at least a glimpse on everything that stays offstage regarding how the war changed our lives and the way we cope. Volunteers are simple ordinary people, who have jobs, and families and all the routine, and yet they find time to think, to help, to buy, to send, to organise, to ask, and search, and find, and deliver just because our freedom, the democracy itself, our integrity is our shared responsibility and the way we show up is our personal responsibility.

So, why did I write this book? To open the hearts of more and more people to compassion and personal responsibility, to inspire more and more people to think about our global community as one family. We are all one. The harm that is being done to one part of our family influences everyone. And while a big aim seems hard to accomplish, it's always the first step that brings us closer to it. So, becoming leaders in our own areas of responsibilities, being mindful and open-hearted right through the daily tasks, bringing our talents to light and being willing to serve – we are making this world a better place, stepping into new knowledge of our capabilities.

Such stories crack us open from inside to realise how fragile this life is. There is no small act of kindness. And that act of kindness, that compassion, those words of support, impulses to make a change in this world are kind of urgent,